This edition first published in 2005 by
Sea-to-Sea Publications
1980 Lookout Drive
North Mankato
Minnesota 56003

ISBN   1-932889-25-6

Printed in China

Library of Congress Control Number: 2004103720

2 4 6 8 9 7 5 3

Published by arrangement with the Watts Publishing Group Ltd, London

Author: Rachel Wright
Modelmaker: Ivan Bulloch
Designed by Victoria Illiffe
Illustrated by Michael Evans
Photography by John Englefield
Edited by Matthew Parselle

Series editor: Paula Borton
Series designer: Robert Walster

LOOK AND MAKE

PRESENTS

SEA-TO-SEA
Mankato Collingwood London

Getting ready

Before you start making your presents, read all the instructions carefully and check that you have everything you need.

On the opposite page you can see the general things you will need. You can find these around your home or in most craft supply stores.

Be prepared

Cover your work area with plenty of old newspaper. Wear an apron or an old shirt and roll up your sleeves.

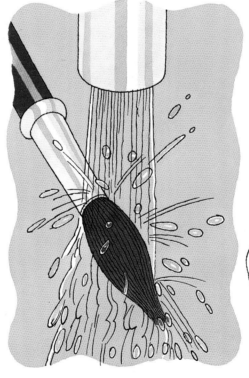

When you have finished, rinse your brushes and put the lids back on your felt-tip markers.

Be very careful when using scissors. If you find anything tricky to cut, ask an adult to help you.

You will need

Here are the things you will need most often when you make the presents in this book.

ready-mix paint

round-ended scissors

ribbon

colored construction paper

ruler

glue stick

felt-tip markers

white glue

pencils

paintbrushes

tissue paper

Animal bookmarks

You will need:

colored construction paper

glue stick

These would make an excellent present for a bookworm.

Try making other animal bookmarks.

Octopus

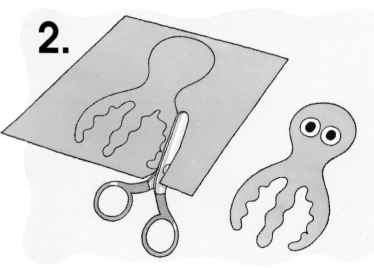

1. Draw an octopus with long tentacles. Copy this one.

2. Cut out the octopus carefully. Add big eyes.

Elephant

1.

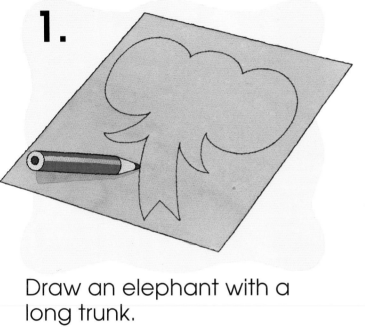

Draw an elephant with a long trunk.

2.

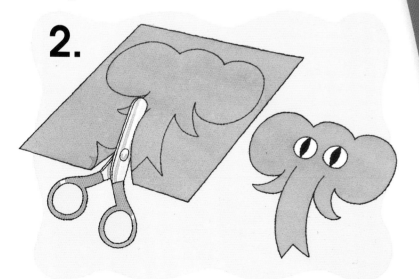

Cut around the elephant. Cut slits either side of its trunk. Add eyes.

Slide your bookmark over a page in a book.

Bright beads

You will need:

a long piece
of thin ribbon

colored
construction
paper

glue stick

1.

Draw lots of long, thin strips on the colored paper with a ruler.

2.

Cut along the lines. Roll one of the strips around a pencil.

3.

Glue down the edge of the strip. Now carefully slide out the pencil.

*These would make
a great present for
a big sister.*

*Try adding
wooden beads
bought from a store.*

4.

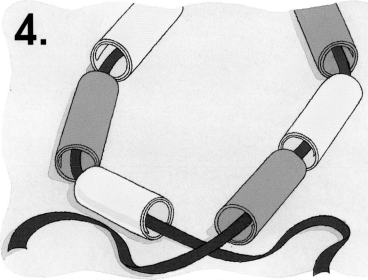

Make more beads. Thread them
onto the ribbon and tie the ends.

Hanging flowers

You will need:

colored tissue paper

paper plate

adhesive tape

two long ribbons

glue stick

This flower would make a pretty present for Mother's Day.

colored construction paper

1.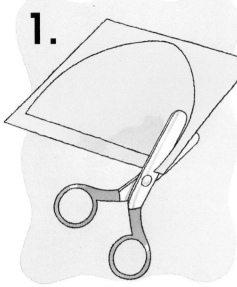

Draw a large petal on the construction paper. Cut it out.

2.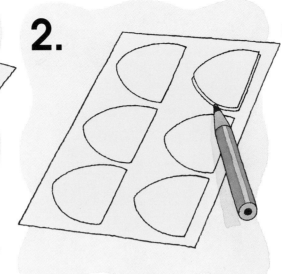

Draw around the petal six times. Cut out all the petals.

3.

Stick the petals to the back of the paper plate as shown here.

4.

Tear the tissue paper into squares and crunch them up tightly into balls.

5.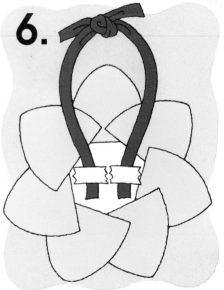

Stick the balls to the front of the plate. Use lots of colors. Cover the whole plate.

6.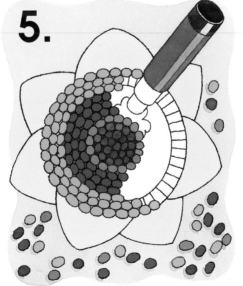

Tape one end of each ribbon to the back of the plate. Tie the ends.

9

Starry stationery

You will need:

plain writing paper
and envelopes

paints

a piece of thin
cardboard

paper
towels

small piece
of sponge

*Tie a piece of ribbon around
your stationery to make a
lovely present.*

1.

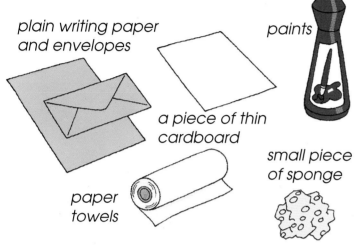

Fold the piece of card in half.
Draw half a star on one side.

Try some other shapes.

2.

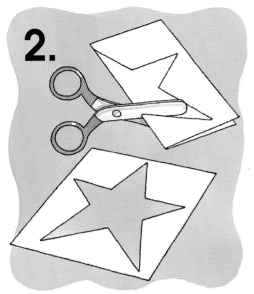

Cut the star out through both sides. Open the card out to make your stencil.

3.

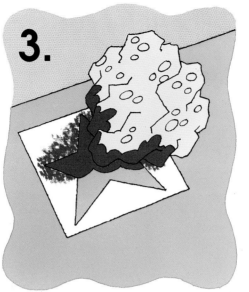

Hold your stencil firmly on your writing paper. Dab on paint with the sponge.

4.

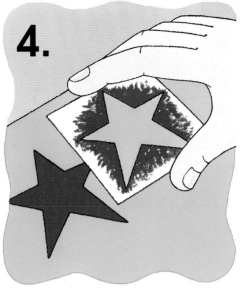

Carefully lift off your stencil. Wipe it dry with some paper towel to use it again.

Decorate your envelopes in the same way.

Paper vase

You will need:

colored paper

white glue

old cup (to mix the glue in)

water

old jar (or glass)

paintbrush

Fill your vase with flowers to make a beautiful present.

12

1.

Cut or tear lots of different colored pieces of paper.

2.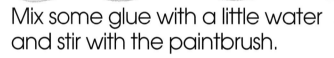

Mix some glue with a little water and stir with the paintbrush.

3.

Stick the pieces of paper to the jar with the watery glue.

4.

The glue is clear when dry.

Varnish the jar with white glue. Then leave it to dry.

Clown frieze

You will need:

a long piece of thin colored cardboard

glue stick

scraps of colored construction paper

ruler

Ask an adult to stick your frieze to your baby brother or sister's bedroom wall.

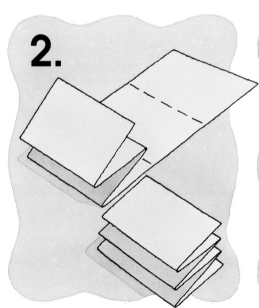

1. Divide the long piece of paper into six equal parts with the ruler and pencil.

2. Fold the paper back and forth along the lines to make a fan shape.

3. Draw a clown shape on the top fold. Make sure its hands and feet touch the edges.

4.

Cut around the clown. Then open the paper out to make a chain of clowns.

5.

Decorate the clowns with paper hats, eyes, bow ties, buttons, and anything else you like.

Desk organizer

This will make a useful present for an untidy person!

You will need:

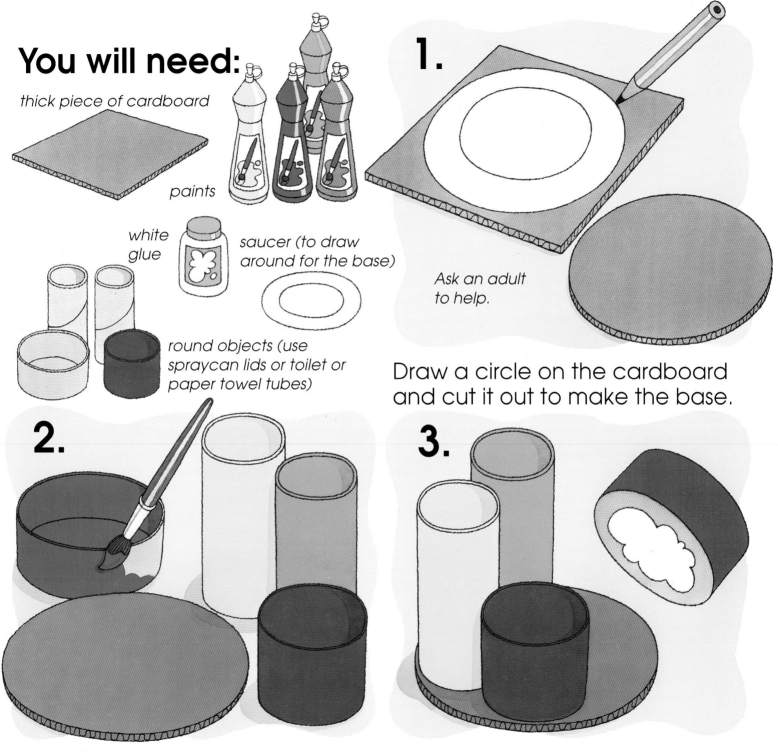

thick piece of cardboard

paints

white glue

saucer (to draw around for the base)

round objects (use spraycan lids or toilet or paper towel tubes)

1.

Ask an adult to help.

Draw a circle on the cardboard and cut it out to make the base.

2.

Paint the base and the round objects with thick paint.

3.

Leave to dry. Then glue the objects to the base.

17

Tissue eggs

You will need:

one or more eggs

white glue

scraps of colored tissue paper

small bowl

thick needle

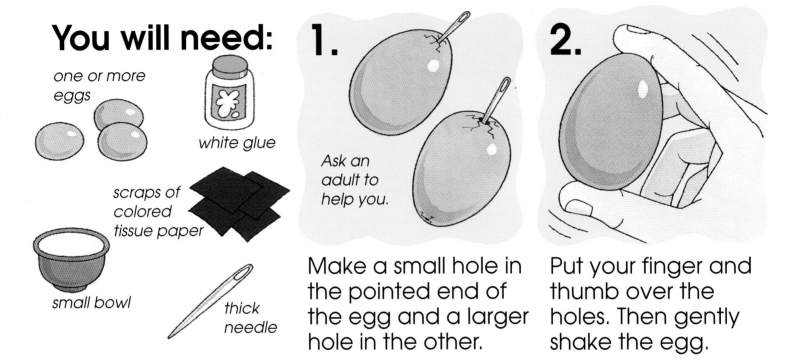

1. Ask an adult to help you.

Make a small hole in the pointed end of the egg and a larger hole in the other.

2.

Put your finger and thumb over the holes. Then gently shake the egg.

3.

Blow hard into the small hole. Shake the egg and blow again until it is empty.

4.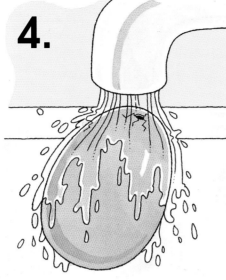

Rinse it under a faucet. Blow through the bigger hole and wipe the egg dry.

5. *The tissue paper will cover any cracks.*

Glue scraps of tissue paper to the egg. Smooth them down gently with your fingers.

You could put your eggs in a basket filled with tissue paper.

6. *The glue is clear when dry.*

Cover the egg with tissue. Leave to dry. Then varnish it with watery white glue.

19

Scrapbook

You will need:

thin colored
cardboard

colored
construction
paper

pieces of ribbon
(or string)

hole punch

1.

Draw and cut out two rectangles of thin cardboard both the same size to make the covers of the book.

2.

Draw around one of the covers on some construction paper.

3.

Cut out the rectangle to make a page. Make lots of pages.

4.

Hold the covers and the pages together and punch holes in one side.

5.

Thread the ribbon through the holes and tie your scrapbook together.

Decorate the cover of your scrapbook.

Fiona's
Scrapbook

You could write your friend's name on the cover.

Name snake

You will need:

empty matchboxes (one for each letter of your friend's name and one extra for the head)

glue stick

short strips of ribbon

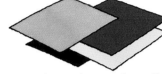
colored construction paper

felt-tip marker

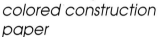
adhesive tape

1.

Cut out pieces of colored construction paper long enough to wrap around the matchboxes. Put the paper to one side.

Add red paper stripes.

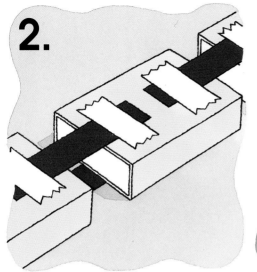

2.

Join the matchboxes together by taping the strips of ribbon on the tops and bottoms.

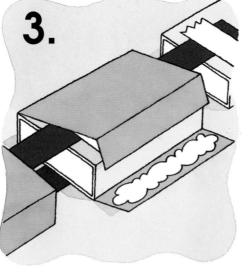

3.

Wrap the colored paper around each matchbox and glue down the edge.

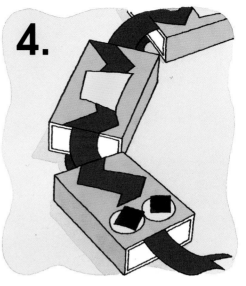

4.

Decorate your snake. Add eyes, a tongue, and paper squares to write on.

This would make a fun present for a friend. Write the letters of their name in the letter squares.

You could put candies inside each matchbox as a surprise.

Pencil aliens

You will need:

pen

pencil crayons

white glue

sponge cloths

1. Put the end of a pencil on a piece of cloth. Draw an alien face around it and cut it out.

2. Draw around the shape onto another cloth and cut out a second face.

3. Cut out some alien ears. Glue them onto one face shape.

24

4.

Glue the edges of one face, leaving the end free. Press the other piece on top.

5.

Cut out cloth eyes and a nose and glue them on. Leave your alien to dry.

This family of pencil aliens would make a playful present for a brother or sister.

Slide your alien on top of a pencil.

Soccer key-ring

You will need:

cookie sheet

wire cooling rack

mixing bowl

knife

acrylic paints

wooden spoon

thin ribbon

2 cups of salt

2 cups of all-purpose flour, plus a little extra

1 cup of warm water

rolling pin

white glue

1. Mix the flour, salt, and warm water together in the bowl.

Before you begin, preheat your oven to 300°F.

Line your cookie sheet with foil.

2. Cover your fingers with flour. Mix and squeeze the mixture with your hands until it forms a soft ball of dough.

3. Sprinkle flour on a surface and the rolling pin. Roll out the dough until it is about as thick as a pencil.

4.

Cut a circle from the dough.
Use a glass to cut around.
Make a hole near the edge.

5.

*See the box in the bottom left.
Ask an adult to help.*

Bake the dough
for about an hour.
Leave it to cool.

This will make a great present for your dad.

Try making a car key-ring.

6.

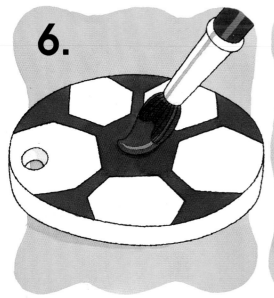

Paint on soccer
colors. Let it dry.
Then paint it again
and leave it to dry.

7.

The glue is clear when dry.

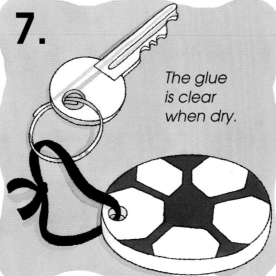

Paint the ball with white glue
to varnish it. Let it dry. Thread
the ribbon through the hole
and tie it to a key.

Wrapping paper

You will need:

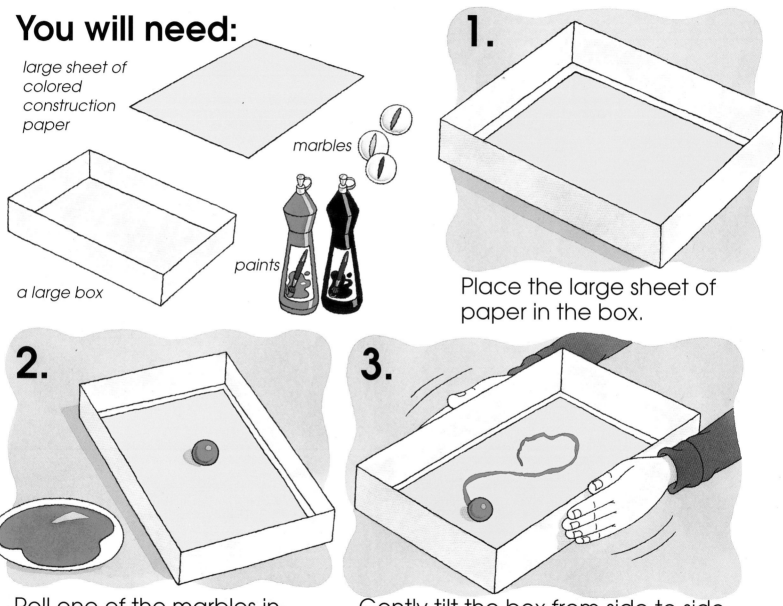

large sheet of colored construction paper

marbles

paints

a large box

1.

Place the large sheet of paper in the box.

2.

Roll one of the marbles in some watery paint. Then place it on the paper.

3.

Gently tilt the box from side to side to make the marble roll around and make a pattern.

Try flicking paint from a paintbrush onto your paper for a different effect.

4.

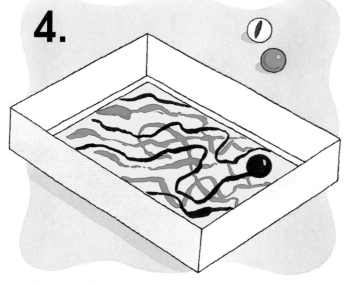

Take the marble out and repeat steps 2 and 3 with different colors.

How to wrap a gift

You will need:

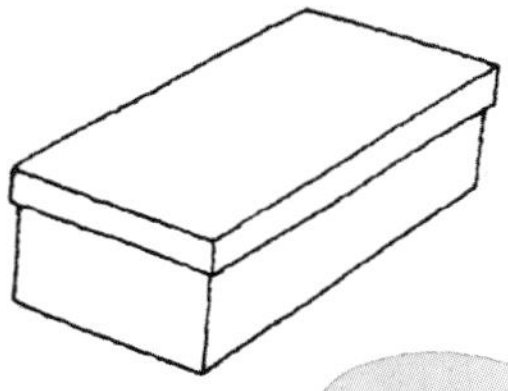

a present
in a box

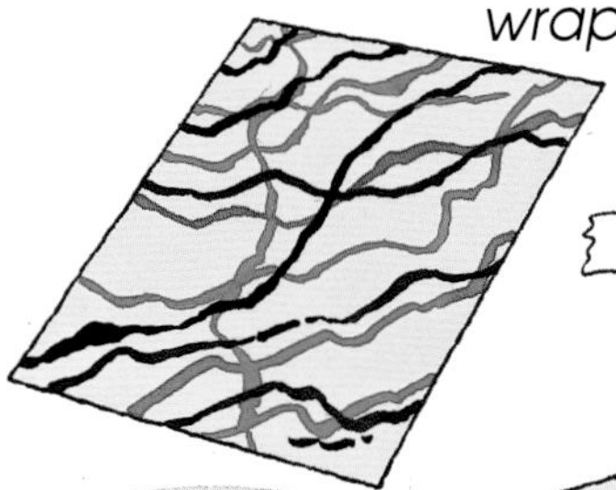

wrapping paper

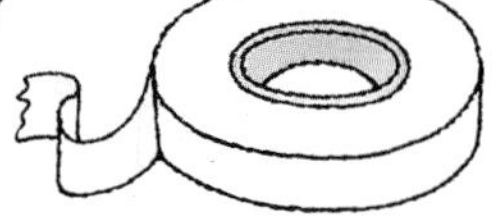

adhesive tape

1.

Cut a piece of wrapping paper
longer and wider than the present.

Tie a big ribbon
around your present.

Turn the page to see
how to make the
gift tags.

2.

Fold the wrapping paper over the present as shown. Tape down the top edge.

3.

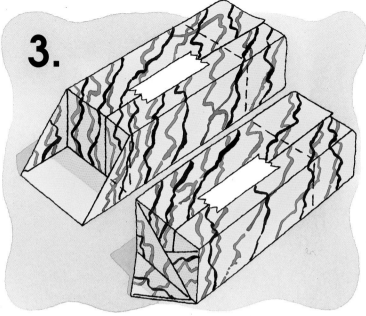

Tuck down one end of the paper. Fold in the flaps on each side so that they form a point.

4.

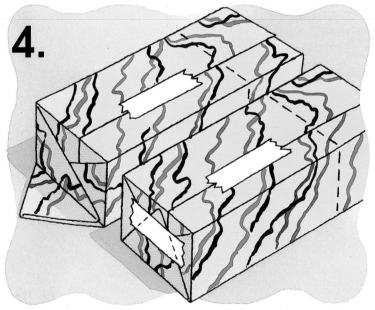

Stick the pointed flap of paper to the side of the present with adhesive tape.

5.

Turn the present around and repeat steps 3 and 4 for the other end of the present.

31

Jazzy gift tags

You will need:

a small piece of thin colored cardboard

wool (or thin ribbon)

hole punch (or a pencil point)

adhesive tape

1.

Draw a bell shape on the paper. Cut it out and punch a hole in the top.

2.

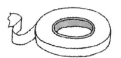

Make as many gift tags as you need.

Thread the wool through the hole as shown.

3.

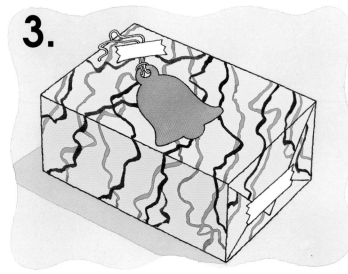

Write your message on one side of the tag and stick it to the present.

Index